START HERE

START HERE

A Teacher's Handbook of
Stories and Themes from the Bible

Scottish
Committee

BLACKIE

Blackie & Son Ltd
Bishopbriggs
Glasgow G65 2NZ

7 Leicester Place
London WC2H 7BP

First published 1983
ISBN 0 216 91696 8

Printed in Great Britain by
Thomson Litho Ltd, East Kilbride, Scotland

PREFACE

Start Here has been compiled largely because as practising teachers and Christians we have been concerned that Religious Education seems to have failed to find a proper place in the organized curriculum of many schools, especially Primary schools. This is despite the many helpful books already on the market and the many excellent radio and television school broadcasts. In our discussions with teachers we have come to the conclusion that instead of helping, these materials often bewilder, partly in their variety and partly in that at times the material appears to have only very tenuous links with R.E.

We therefore felt that a return to basics was necessary and we have presented here stories and themes from both the Old and New Testament which we hope will provide teachers with a basis for teaching a meaningful R.E. programme based on the Bible. However, it is not meant to completely replace other approaches. The stories and themes have been chosen as suitable for children in the age range 5 to 7 and in each case the biblical source is quoted. Even teachers who have little or no knowledge of the Bible can use the stories by reading over the relevant passages beforehand, preferably in a modern version such as the *Good News Bible*.

At the beginning we list the stories both in order of the book and also grouped in themes. The lessons can be done in the order in which they appear or they can be introduced through the themes suggested at appropriate times in the year. The time taken for each lesson will depend on the amount of work the teacher plans to do but for those who wish to develop the stories further either in class or in assembly we have included a number of optional related activities with simple, easy-to-follow sketches for guidance where appropriate.

CONTENTS

These lessons are listed overleaf as topics for teachers who prefer a thematic approach.

A THEMATIC APPROACH USING THE STORIES SELECTED

USEFUL PUBLICATIONS AND PUBLISHERS

We list here some of the books which we use most frequently in our lessons. Not all are still in print but may be found in the resource library.

HYMNS, SONGS AND PRAYERS
1. *The Church Hymnary*   (O.U.P.)
2. *Someone's Singing, Lord*   (Black)
3. *Apusskidu*   (Black)
4. *Come and Sing*   (Scripture Union)
5. *Come and Praise*   (B.B.C. Publications)
6. *Sing to God*   (Scripture Union)
7. *The Nursery Song and Picture Book*   (Religious Educ. Press)
8. *Hymns and Songs*   (Ladybird)
9. *Book of Prayers*   (Ladybird)

BIBLE STORIES AND CHARACTERS
1. Ladybird Books
2. Arch Books
3. Lion Publications
4. Scripture Union
5. Religious Education Press
6. 'Read About it' series   (Wheaton)
7. National Bible Society Publications for Children
8. Frances Hook *Present Day Pictures*   (N.C.E.C.)
9. *A Child's Story of Jesus*   (Dean)
10. *Children's Bible Stories*   (Dean)

GENERAL REFERENCE
1. Blackwell's Learning Library
2. *The Bible Stories Retold*   Margaret McCrea   (Evans)
3. *Religious Education, Primary School Handbook*   (Scottish Joint Committee on Religious Education)
4. *Living Light*   (Holmes McDougall)
5. The How and Why Books   (Transworld)
6. Philip's *Pictorial Atlas of the Bible*
7. *Learning About Religion*   (Schofield and Sims)
8. *Life in Bible Times*   (Chambers)
9. *Who? What? Where? in the Bible*   (Blackie)

OLD
TESTAMENT

GOD'S WONDERFUL WORLD

Genesis 1

AIM

To evoke in children a sense of wonder and joy in God's created things.

1. Children will be introduced to some of the various aspects of God's creation by sensory experience; by singing, drama and handwork, and by being involved in stories.
2. They will come first to appreciate God's world and then to care for created things.
3. An emotional response to beauty and a desire to worship will be aroused.

INTRODUCTION

Throughout the development of the theme, children will be involved with the class nature table, and the classroom should reflect the theme in pictures, models and friezes. Nature books should be available. Songs and hymns should be learned. Prayers should be displayed beside appropriate pictures, etc. A personal "book" with a title like "My Book of God's Wonderful World" could include drawings, prayers, etc. Compose a class version of "My Favourite Things"—tune from "The Sound of Music".

SUGGESTED BOOKS AND MATERIALS

1. Modern version of the Bible, e.g. *Good News Bible*.
2. *Religious Education, Primary School Handbook* (Scottish Joint Committee on Religious Education).
3. Frances Hook *Present Day Pictures* (N.C.E.C.)
4. *Someone's Singing, Lord* and *The Church Hymnary*.
5. Ladybird Nature Books, *Book of Prayers* and *Hymns and Songs*.
6. Filmstrips, e.g. "All Things Bright and Beautiful" dealing with wind, water, fire, etc.

Lesson 1   Sun, Moon and Stars

SUGGESTED PROCEDURE

1. Pictures of a sunny day and of a stormy night sky.
   (a) Discuss qualities of the sun—light, heat, makes things grow, can be hidden by clouds.
   (b) Discuss night-time—sun is not shining but moon and stars are; time when animals and birds sleep. Mention one or two nocturnal creatures; time when people sleep. Mention nurses, firemen, policemen, who stay awake to help us if we need them.
   (c) Using pictures return to the moon and stars. Moon looks bigger than the stars because it is nearer. Moon goes round the earth each month, changes its shape and even disappears but it will come back again.

(d) Likewise the stars are always there, though on a cloudy night we may not see them. Children may learn to recognize the Milky Way, the Plough and Pole Star.

2. Men have always looked at the stars and keep looking for new ones.

3. God's Creation: Genesis 1:14–19; Psalm 8:3; Psalm 136:7–9; Psalm 148:3.

OPTIONAL ACTIVITIES

1. Prayer: We thank you, God, for the sun during the day and the moon and the stars at night. Help us to remember that you made them to tell us of your love and care for us.

2. Frieze: A sunny day, the moon and stars at night—caption from verse 3 of "God, who made the earth".

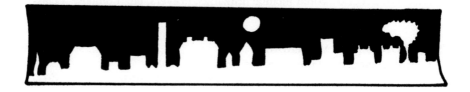

3. Book: Children can begin personal "Wonderful World" book.

4. Groups: Can make their own "Sky at Night".

5. Sing: "God, who made the earth", "God who put the stars in space" (both from *The Church Hymnary*), "Twinkle, twinkle little star" (*Someone's Singing, Lord*).

Lesson 2   Animals

SUGGESTED PROCEDURE

1. Discussion could centre round:
   - (a) Pets and their care
   - (b) Farmyard animals
   - (c) Wild animals—including hibernation, etc.
   - (d) Animals which help us—sheepdogs, guidedogs, etc.

   Pictures on the above topics are readily available or class books or displays from cut-outs could be made.
2. Stories: *The Incredible Journey*; *Greyfriars Bobby*.
3. God's Creation: Genesis 1:24.

OPTIONAL ACTIVITIES

1. Prayer: Thank you, heavenly Father, for all the lovely creatures you have made, especially for our pets. Help us to take care of them and help us always to be kind and gentle to them.
   or Ladybird *Book of Prayers*, page 16 or 30.
2. Frieze: Make animals to go on a frieze with caption from the hymn "God who made all things".

3. Book: Children could draw their favourite animals for their own book.
4. Sing: "All things bright and beautiful" *(The Church Hymnary)*.

Lesson 3   Birds

SUGGESTED PROCEDURE

1. (a) Look at pictures, including R.S.P.B. pictures.
   (b) Listen to a tape of birdsong.
   (c) Observe birds in the playground, pet birds, birds in the garden, migration.
2. Story about animals.
3. God's Creation: Genesis 1:26; Matthew 6:26.

OPTIONAL ACTIVITIES

1. Prayer: Father we thank you for the birds that sing and make us happy. Help people to look after them in the winter time. Help people to enjoy the birds they see and hear and not to hurt them.
   or Ladybird *Book of Prayers*, page 42, "Our friends the birds".
2. Continue personal book and frieze under the heading "God who made all things". Using tissue paper, make brightly-coloured birds.
3. Sing: "Morning has broken", "This is a lovely world", "Little birds in winter time", "All things bright and beautiful" (all from *Someone's Singing, Lord*).

Lesson 4   Flowers

SUGGESTED PROCEDURE

1. (a) Make full use of the nature table to draw attention to the various colours of flowers in different seasons, bulbs in the classroom, winter twigs, snowdrops, etc.
   (b) Teach the names of common flowers and the main parts of flowers.
   (c) Discuss the fact that, like birds and animals, flowers have needs too—water, sun, plant food and good soil, shelter, etc. Do not pick wild flowers unnecessarily.

   (d) Pleasure from flowers—gifts, displays, etc.
   (e) Harvest Festivals and displays could be a good introduction.
2. Unless you have a story you wish to tell, omit this element and substitute drama. Mime the tiny seed, growing to a big flower and spreading out. Mime the open flower in the sunlight and the closed flower at night.
3. God's Creation: Genesis 1:11–12, 31; Matthew 6:28–9.

OPTIONAL ACTIVITIES

1. Prayer: For the colours of the flowers
   For the colours of birds and butterflies
   For eyes to see colour everywhere
   We thank you our Father.

   or Ladybird *Book of Prayers* has many examples, e.g. page 26.

2. Arrange the classroom with beautiful flowers and plants.

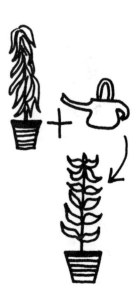

3. Continue with own books and frieze.
4. Sing: "All things bright and beautiful", "Think of a world without any flowers", "All the flowers are waking", "The flowers that grow in the garden" (all from *Someone's Singing, Lord*).

Lesson 5   Wind and Rain

SUGGESTED PROCEDURE

1. Class weather chart. Infant pictures of windy and rainy days. (Try to teach this lesson on such a day.)

Mon.	☀	🌂	🌂	☁
Tues.	☁☀	☀	☀	☁
Wed.	☁	💨☁	☀	🌂
Thurs.	🌂	☀	☁☀	☁
Fri.	☁	☀	🌂	☀

2. (a) Listen to music which suggests wind and storm.
   (b) The rain wets flowers and leaves so that they shine in the sun (also grow better—recapitulate flower lesson). We can see our reflections in puddles.

7

(c) The trees and flowers wave in the wind; leaves scurry along; kites fly; yachts sail fast; seeds are dispersed.

(d) Mime the wind blowing different objects. Use water in the classroom to show boats sailing (made with matchbox and paper).

NOTE   As with flowers, no specific story is offered as this is a "feeling" lesson—affective more than cognitive teaching to make children appreciate that windy and rainy days are God's good gifts too. If desired, tell any story of children secure at home while there is wind and rain outside.

3. God's Creation: Genesis 9:12–17. The rainbow and its promise. Emphasis on joy—the rainbow as a symbol of God's love and presence with us in all situations.

OPTIONAL ACTIVITIES

1. Prayer: We thank you Father for the wind, the rain, the sun.
   We thank you for clothes to keep us warm and dry.
   We thank you that we can have fun in the wind and the rain.
2. Continue with books and frieze. Make own rainbows.
3. Sing: "We thank you, God, for eyes to see" *(The Church Hymnary)*.

Lesson 6   Eyes and Ears

SUGGESTED PROCEDURE

1. Have a collection of attractive things and pleasant-sounding objects, mainly based on previous lessons.
2. (a) Shutting our eyes and listening to noises in and out of classroom develops appreciation of ears. The "feely" bag or passing objects to each other, again with eyes shut, helps appreciation of sight.
   (b) Play guessing game where children mime well-known actions, e.g. cleaning teeth, driving a car, eating ice-creams, etc. Other mimes like a policeman directing traffic, an aeroplane, a cat walking, etc. can be used (teacher can make suggestions to performers) to heighten the understanding of sight.
   (c) Likewise a tape of common sounds can be made or teacher can ask children to make sounds like a bell or tambourine while eyes are closed. Story of Bartimaeus can be told here (Mark 10:46–52), see page 66.
3. God's Creation: Genesis 1:26–31. The idea of all the lovely things God gives us to see and hear.

OPTIONAL ACTIVITIES

1. Prayer: Thank you Father for eyes to see all the lovely things in your world.—(pause) Thank you Father for ears to hear interesting sounds. Help us to enjoy your world and to help others to be happy in it.
   or Ladybird *Hymns and Songs*.
   or "Give to us eyes. Give to us ears. Give to us hands." is a beautiful prayer.
2. Frieze: "Thank you, God".
3. Display any completed frieze, children's books and other articles made or enjoyed during the series.
4. Sing: "God who made the earth", "Hands to work and feet to run", "All things bright and beautiful" (all from *The Church Hymnary*), "Praise to God for things we see" (*Someone's Singing, Lord*).

THE STORY OF NOAH

Genesis 6:5–9, 17

NOTE   On reading the biblical account of the story of Noah, the adult may wonder and find it difficult to explain what happened to those not in the ark. Why did God allow only one family to be saved? For this reason, some infant teachers prefer to leave it out. The authors, however, feel that this is a well-known story around which stories and songs have been written and illustrations made and that many teachers will be able to use the guidelines provided.

AIM

To tell the story of Noah and the Flood, and relate it to God's caring for, and promises to His people.
1. Children will learn of God's displeasure at what men were doing to the world.
2. They will learn of God's care for creation.
3. They will learn of Noah's faithfulness to God and his obedience.

INTRODUCTION

Talk about rainbows; what they look like and why and when they appear. Ask the children if they know where the rainbow is mentioned in the Bible. Read the verses from Genesis 9:14–15, and tell them that this is the end of a story about a man called Noah.

SUGGESTED PROCEDURE

1. Talk about "God's Wonderful World". Go over some of the points in the previous set of lessons. Talk about the need to care for one another and for all the things around us.
2. Although God had given all these wonderful things for everyone to enjoy, people in Noah's time wasted and spoiled them.
3. Only one man and his family cared about what God said. His name was Noah.
4. Explain that God was going to send a great flood and told Noah to build a big boat on dry land. This was a strange thing to do and all the people laughed at him.
5. Noah gave everyone the chance to go into the Ark but they refused. They laughed when he started to load it up with animals.
6. Talk about the rain which came after the doors were closed and lasted for 40 days. Build up the story of Noah's sending out birds to look for dry land and the eventual landing of the Ark on top of Mount Ararat. The first thing they did when they disembarked was to thank God for saving their lives.
7. Tell of God's promise in the form of the rainbow.

Mr Noah

feltpen   wool

paper bag

OPTIONAL ACTIVITIES

1. Prayer: Help us to look after what you have made for us and help us to obey you and trust you. May we remember your promises every time we see a rainbow.
2. Learn the songs: "Red and Yellow, Pink and Green" (*Apusskidu*, No. 5); "Who Built the Ark?" (*Someone's Singing, Lord,* No. 44); "Mr Noah Built an Ark".
3. Wall frieze of animals going into the ark, rainbows, etc.

4. Story: *I Wish I Lived When Noah Did* by Geoffrey Bull (Pickering & Inglis).
5. Make a Mr Noah's Book.

THE STORY OF JOSEPH

Genesis 37, 39 and 41–7

The story of Joseph occupies several chapters of Genesis. It has all the appeal of the little-one-who-comes-out-on-top and there is much in it with which children can identify.

With Infants the emphasis is best laid on the family aspect, so in this unit the years in Egypt are passed over quickly.

AIM

To tell the story of Joseph. To explore family relationships. To build up in the children's minds a picture of the semi-nomadic lifestyle that provides the background to the early Old Testament stories.

INTRODUCTION

Teachers should familiarize themselves with the history of Joseph, particularly as told in Genesis.

Lesson 1   Joseph's Home

Genesis 37: 1–11

Bring out the following points:

1. Joseph's father Jacob (also called Israel, but this can wait until the children are older) was an important man in the land of Canaan. He had a large family of twelve sons and one daughter. Take out thirteen children one by one and show where Joseph came in—second youngest. Compare with class graph of family sizes. It's worth mentioning the names of Reuben (the eldest), Simeon, Judah, and the youngest, Benjamin. Their sister was Dinah, in case the girls are curious!

2. They were semi-nomads, living in tents but cultivating land as well as rearing large flocks of sheep and goats. The tents were made from black strips of woven goat-hair and were divided into two compartments, one, the men's, used for entertaining, and the other, the women's used for cooking. Describe in detail their way of life, and their work in the fields and with the flocks.

3. Relationships in the home were less than ideal. The brothers were jealous of Joseph because of their father's favouritism, made explicit by the gift of the "coat of many colours", which they may have taken as a sign that he intended Joseph to be his heir. Doubtless they knew also that Joseph kept their father informed of their none-too-creditable deeds. His brothers probably saw Joseph as a spoiled boy who told tales and they hated him for this.

So Joseph's home-life (like that of some of our pupils) had much to make him unhappy, though it was not one of unmitigated misery. There was love in it too—his father's and presumably Benjamin's. All this deserves discussion.

Talk about jealousy, telling tales, etc. Jealousy in families and among friends. How do we deal with it? Help children to realize that everyone has good points and gifts as well as bad points. We're all different. Nowhere in the Bible does God deal with "ideal" people.

4. The dreams (reflecting the work in the fields and the night sky so familiar to desert-dwellers) were the last straw and earned Joseph the bitter nickname of "the Dreamer". In those days dreams (or some of them) were taken very seriously, and although he rebuked his son, Jacob nevertheless took note of the dreams and remembered them.

Tell the dreams and invite the children to guess whom the sheaves might represent. Ask them what they think the brothers' reaction will be. "Who does he think he is?" they might well ask. "They hated him even more for his dreams and for his words" (verse 8).

OPTIONAL ACTIVITIES

1. Prayer: Lord, help us.

    We don't want to be jealous of other people.

    We don't want to make our friends jealous of us.

    Help us to love and care for our friends and families.

2. Language: Children may want to talk about their dreams. They could tell them to the class or tape them. For children who suffer from night-mares it can be therapeutic to talk freely and matter-of-factly about them. The exercise of finding words to describe them seems to take some of the terror out of them.

    It could be pointed out that, by and large, our dreams are just dreams and mean nothing. On the other hand, in Joseph's time, God sometimes spoke to people through dreams.

3. Movement: Act the dreams to music. This is an opportunity to introduce some classical music—perhaps part of Beethoven's 6th Symphony (the "Pastoral") or part of the Moonlight Sonata.

For the first dream, to make sheaves, cut a child-high strip of yellow crepe paper, at 10 cm intervals, from the bottom up to shoulder height, and likewise from the top down to the neck and tie one round each child gathering it at the neck.

yellow crepe paper

cut

Joseph's Dreams

For the second dream, cut a large sun, moon and stars and decorate with foil or paint. Make two slits so that the child can push his hands through and get a grip so as to hold it in front of himself; or draw a simple picture.

4. Art:
   (a) Begin a frieze showing milestones in Joseph's life, e.g.:
      (i) At home working in the fields with his brothers, or tents against a night sky with the family safe inside asleep (and dreaming!).
      (ii) Joseph in his coat going to meet his brothers.
      (iii) In the pit.
      (iv) In Potiphar's house.
      (v) Reunited with his family.

   Have the children look up the reiterated phrase, "The Lord was with Joseph" (Chapter 39, verse 2, 3 and 21) and write it above the frieze with ribbons linking it to each episode. Alternatively each child, or group, could make a book about Joseph with a picture and sentence(s) on each page.

   (b) Joseph's coat has captured the imagination of countless children (and adults). Discuss fully the dress of men and women of the time. Whether Joseph's "coat" was the outer cloak or the tunic worn beneath it, is not certain. It may have been checked, striped, patchwork or embroidered. Either give the children a cut-out each to design, or do one life-size coat to which all contribute, e.g. a patch of paper or cloth for a patchwork coat. If a simple semi-circular shape is used with a small semi-circle cut out for the head, children can have fun wearing it.

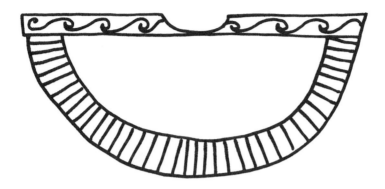

Lesson 2   Sold into Slavery

Genesis 37:12–35

AIM

To show that God was with Joseph in very difficult circumstances, and to help children realize that He cares for them too.

INTRODUCTION

Remind the children of Joseph's home circumstances.

SUGGESTED PROCEDURE

Tell the next episode in Joseph's life:

1. The brothers went in search of fresh pastures for their sheep and goats.
2. Jacob sent Joseph to see how they were getting on. Describe his journey; initial lack of success, wanderings, and how he was directed by the man he met.
3. Tell about the brothers' "welcome"—their plot to kill him, Reuben's suggestion that they leave him in a pit to die and Joseph's anguish and pleading as they stripped him of his coat and threw him into the pit (meant for storing water but now mercifully dry).
4. At Judah's suggestion they sold him to passing traders.
5. The brothers now had the problem of what to tell their father. Perhaps some of the children know how they solved it. Their deception of their father highlights the heartlessness of these men, and Joseph, years later, had good reason to test them before revealing himself to them.

Conclusion: Point out that, though it looked as if the brothers were having everything their own way, in reality God was in charge and He was taking care of Joseph—in the pit and on his way to Egypt too.

OPTIONAL ACTIVITIES

1. Prayer: Lord, we thank You for Your love. When we are afraid help us to remember that You are with us. Amen.
2. Act out the scene or mime it.
    (a) Jacob sends Joseph to his brothers.
    (b) He is redirected by the friendly stranger.
    (c) The brothers see him coming and plot to kill him.
    (d) Joseph is thrown into the pit.
    (e) Reuben goes off to round up some sheep while the others sit down to have a picnic.
    (f) Traders arrive on their camels and Joseph is sold for 20 pieces of silver.

    (g) Reuben returns.
    (h) The bloodstained coat is shown to Jacob.
3. Continue the frieze or booklets.
4. Sing: "God is always near me" (*The Church Hymnary*).

Lesson 3   Joseph in Egypt

Genesis 39:1–6

AIM

To show God's continuing care of Joseph. To help the children to realize that they, too, may depend on God's interest and concern in their lives.

INTRODUCTION

Recapitulate the story so far by reading Genesis 37:3–35. It's good to let them see that the story comes from the Bible and this passage is easy to understand.

SUGGESTED PROCEDURE
Describe the next stage in Joseph's life.

1. *The Journey*
   Ask the children to imagine how Joseph felt as he rode with strangers, whose speech he didn't understand, to an unknown destination. What were his thoughts and feelings? There's one thing he could do. Suggest that he may have prayed to God to be with him. What, specifically, might he have asked of God? (A kind master, comfort for his father, a forgiving attitude, to bring him home again . . .)

2. *The Marketplace*
   Describe an Eastern market—the jostling, the clamour, the stalls with their variety of goods (e.g. baskets at one, goats at another, fruit at the next, slaves at yet another, etc.). That's where Joseph was taken—to be sold just like something you'd buy in a shop.

3. *Potiphar*
   As he stood there, apprehensively watching the buyers, he noticed a tall man approach—an Egyptian of military bearing. He overheard him haggling with the stallholder. Eventually Joseph was handed over for a sum of money. (Plenty of scope for imaginative detail here!) Potiphar, captain of Pharaoh's guard, took him to his lovely house. He was lucky. (Do the children think God knew?) He worked hard, pleased his master and prospered. Discuss what his duties might have been. Not only did he please Potiphar; he pleased God too, and God was with him.

OPTIONAL ACTIVITIES
1. Copy out Genesis 39:5.
   "The Lord blessed the Egyptian's house for Joseph's sake".
   They could decorate the edges of their paper with hieroglyphic-style markings.
2. Continue the frieze or booklets.
3. Act the scene in the marketplace with stallholders bawling their wares, buyers haggling over prices, and Potiphar looking over the slaves before bargaining for Joseph.

Lesson 4   Reunited!

Genesis 41:54 to 47:12 or summary in 50:15–21

AIM
To show God's continuing care of Joseph, culminating in the reunion with his family.
To show that behind events there is a God who cares and is in control.

INTRODUCTION
Remind the children of Joseph's position in Potiphar's house.

SUGGESTED PROCEDURE
Pass over the ensuing years and go on to tell of the reconciliation with his family. It is probably best not to go into all the ramifications of Joseph's testing of his brothers but to give a condensed version somewhat as follows. Salient points are:

1. *Joseph the Prime Minister*
   Years passed. Joseph was now Prime Minister of Egypt, living in a large house, rich and busy.

2. *Years of Famine*
   There was famine. People came from far and wide to buy food in Egypt where there was plenty. Joseph was in charge of the stores.

3. *Meeting with the Brothers*
   One day ten men arrived. As they entered they bowed low. (Does this remind the children of something?) Joseph started asking them questions. He recognized them, but they didn't recognize him. Guess who they were. He asked, "Is your father still alive?" For whom would he also ask. (Do the class remember the name of his young brother?) Joseph said, "Go back home and bring Benjamin with you next time". When they came back with Benjamin, Joseph told them who he was and said, "Now go back and bring my father and the rest of the family and we shall all live in Egypt together".

4. *The Reunion*

The family was together once more. Describe graphically their joy; especially Jacob's at seeing his son again; Joseph's at seeing his father; the brothers' at being forgiven.

Bring out the fact that God had been watching over Joseph and his family all the time.

OPTIONAL ACTIVITIES

1. Finish the frieze.
2. (a) Act the part of the story covered in Lesson 4.
   (b) Combine the various scenes they have dramatized into a play about Joseph.
   (c) Mime scenes from Joseph's life.

   The story of Joseph could very well he told as part of a project on Egypt. In this case his stay in Egypt would incorporate much more background information than is indicated here.
3. Make up workcards to revise the story.

Dressing Up Box

1. How many were in Jacob's family?
2. What did they live in?
3. Where did they get water?

1. Name Joseph's oldest brother.
2. Draw their home
3. Who looks after sheep?

1. Who was Potiphar?
2. Where did they put Joseph?
3. Who did he meet?

1. Have you seen
1. Draw what is

Workcards about Joseph.

plastic marg. carton

THE CHILD MOSES

Exodus 2

AIM

To tell the story of Moses as a baby and illustrate God's care for him.

INTRODUCTION

1. General discussion about babies, perhaps related to the theme on "Families" (see page viii).
   (a) Ourselves as babies (children could bring in their baby photographs).
   (b) Babies in our home.
   (c) Helping mother to look after baby.

SUGGESTED PROCEDURE

1. Using knowledge of Exodus 2, give background to story. Briefly tell how, many years before, people from Moses' country had gone to live in Egypt (recall previous lesson on Joseph). At that time the king liked them and gave them land to live on but at the time of this story the king was cruel to the Israelites and parents had to hide their babies to keep them safe.
2. Having read Exodus 2, tell the story from Miriam's point of view and emphasize:
   (a) how she longed for Moses to be kept safe.
   (b) what she did to take care of the baby.
   (c) how she felt when the princess appeared.
   (d) how she suggested that his own mother should become his nurse.
3. Tell how he grew up to be strong and healthy as a prince living in the palace and how the princess gave him a special name (see verse 10).

collage with wallpaper scraps

OPTIONAL ACTIVITIES

1. Make up frieze or book of baby Moses and attach own baby pictures.

2. Songs about babies, lullabies, etc.
3. Poem: "Little Baby Moses"

> Rocking gently to and fro,
> Floating in the rushes,
> Sleeping in his cradle boat,
> Little baby Moses.
>
> Miriam, his sister kind,
> Sitting by the rushes,
> Watched the baby all day long,
> Little baby Moses.

(source unknown)

4. Paint or make model of basket in the bulrushes.
5. This story lends itself to acting.

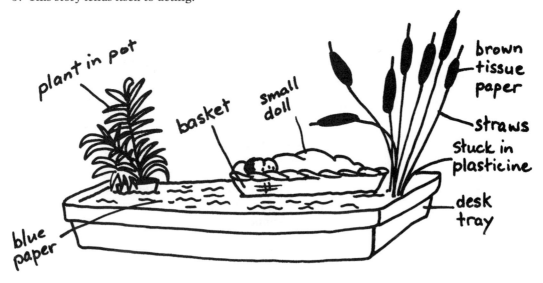

THE BOY SAMUEL

1 Samuel 1:1–28; 2:18–21; 3:1–10

AIM

To tell the story of Samuel and to teach how God hears and answers our prayers. Show that children can serve God.

INTRODUCTION

1. Discuss families and family sizes; perhaps related to the theme on "Families" (see page viii). Refer perhaps to a class graph.
2. Introduce the story of Hannah as found in 1 Samuel 1:1–28.

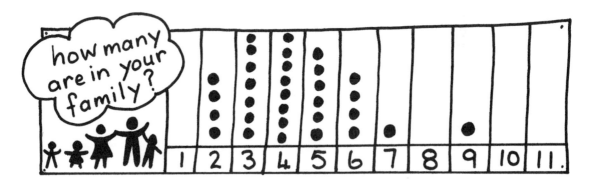

SUGGESTED PROCEDURE

1. Talk about Hannah's unhappiness in having no children in a country where every woman wanted to have a family of her own. Tell how she spoke to God (discuss praying as speaking to God) and promised that, if she had a son, she would let him work for God in the temple. Explain "temple" as a warm, welcoming place where people came, whenever they were in town, to pray or talk to the priest. A light was always burning to remind them it was God's house.

2. Tell how God answered Hannah's prayer and gave her a son whom she called Samuel. It should perhaps be pointed out to children at this point that God *hears* all prayers but sometimes says *No* or is silent to let us work things out for ourselves.

   When Samuel was a baby Hannah looked after him at home but when he was old enough she kept her promise to God and took him to live in the temple. She continued to see him and care for him there. Talk about how important he would feel, having such a job, and how proud he would be wearing his "new coat" (2:18–21).

3. Introduce Eli as the kind elderly man who was the priest (minister) and to whom Samuel was a helper.

4. Talk about Samuel's life in the temple: going to the temple school every day with the other boys to learn to read and write, keeping the lamps burning, polishing and dusting, opening and closing the doors, counting the money from the offerings, etc.

5. Refer to 1 Samuel 3:1–10. Talk about the sounds that Samuel might hear in the night and the requests from Eli when he was lying in bed. Relate the story as told in the Bible about the voice which Samuel heard and how eventually Eli told him to say, "Speak Lord, your servant is listening".

6. God's message to Samuel was terrible and frightening and he had to tell Eli about it. It is probably wiser to leave this part out with Infants and explain simply that God had chosen Samuel to be a leader of His people when he grew up.

OPTIONAL ACTIVITIES

1. Prayer: Lord help us to be like Samuel, to be willing to serve you every day; to be willing to listen to what you have to tell us.

2. Act the story of Samuel lying on his mat, hearing God's voice, etc., the class singing "Hushed was the evening hymn".

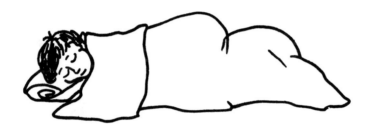

3. Make a frieze showing Samuel doing various jobs in the temple.

4. Sing: "Talking to God", "God hears and answers" *(Come and Sing)* "Hushed was the evening hymn" *(The Church Hymnary)*.

DAVID THE SHEPHERD BOY

1 Samuel 17:12–15, 31–40

AIM

To tell the story of David as a shepherd, emphasizing his faithfulness, his bravery, and God's protection.

INTRODUCTION

1. Describe how David's home might have been: a busy household, noisy and lively with eight sons in the family. David is the youngest; this could be a starting point, asking children to tell what it is like to be the youngest.
2. Talk about task-sharing in a large family. Lead on to David's job as a shepherd. Perhaps relate to the theme on "Families" (see page viii).

SUGGESTED PROCEDURE

1. Talk about what it was like to be a shepherd in Israel. The shepherd had a very close relationship with his sheep. He knew each one, counted them regularly and stayed by them to protect them against wild animals such as lions, bears and wolves.
2. Ask the children what he might think of out there in the hills at night all alone. Would he be afraid? Would he light a fire to keep warm and to frighten wild animals away?
3. Explain how David used to sing and play his harp and make up songs and poems to pass the long hours away. Speak briefly about David the Psalmist and refer perhaps to Psalm 23, "The Lord is my shepherd". Speak about how David felt that God cared for him in the same way that he cared for his father's sheep; sometimes he would be afraid but it helped to know that God was with him.

4. Imaginatively tell the story about the attacks on his sheep by lions and bears. Using his sling, his knife and his rod, he would kill them. Was it worth risking his life for sheep? Yes, because he really cared for them (1 Samuel 17:31–40).

5. Link the above story to God's care for us as children. Though small and alone at times, he cares for us individually.

OPTIONAL ACTIVITIES

1. Prayer: We thank you God that, just as you cared for David the shepherd boy, you care for us every day. Help us to trust you and be faithful to you even when things seem to be going wrong.

2. Sing: "God takes good care of me", "Loving Father of all children" (*Come and Sing*), "The Lord's my shepherd" (*The Church Hymnary*). The latter could also be used as an introduction to the lesson.

3. Drawing, painting, display or frieze of scenes from above stories.

4. Link with sheep and shepherds today.

5. Parable of the Lost Sheep, Luke 15:1–7.

6. Books: *Children of the Bible, The Shepherd Boy of Bethlehem, The Parable of the Lost Sheep* (all Ladybird), *David the Shepherd Boy* (Wheaton), *Life in Bible Times* (Chambers).

DAVID AND GOLIATH

1 Samuel 17

AIM

To tell the story of David and Goliath, and to illustrate how David put his trust in God to help him.

INTRODUCTION

Teachers should familiarize themselves with the story as told in the Bible, in order to tell it graphically. Recall the story of David as a shepherd in the previous lesson. Mention briefly that Israel had enemies, the Philistines, and explain that David's elder brothers were soldiers at that time in the army against them.

SUGGESTED PROCEDURE

1. Explain that King Saul was very unhappy because his army had been losing battles. Now the Philistines had challenged him to choose one man to fight the huge Goliath but no one would do it.
2. David was too young to be in the army but his father sent him to the camp with food for his brothers.
3. Explain that David got to know about the challenge of Goliath and offered to go out and fight him. Everybody laughed at David, even more so when they put some armour on him which nearly knocked him over! Go on to tell of David's persistence and the King's eventual decision to let him meet Goliath after he had heard of his previous bravery as a shepherd.
4. Describe the weapon which David chose; contrast with the catapult which children might know today. Ask children why he was so skilled with this weapon.

Philistine Warrior

leather

5. Paint the picture in words: the opposing armies. David's challenge to Goliath, the two figures facing each other, the mocking of Goliath, the fearlessness of David, etc.
6. Go on to tell of the slingshot, the death of the champion, the cheers from the Israelites and the parading of David as their victor.

7. Conclude by emphasizing the trust which David put in God; his words to Goliath were, "You come to me with a sword, a spear and a shield, but I come to you in the name of the Lord". Explain that even although we often feel weak, God can be with us and give us strength and courage to stand up for what is right and true.

OPTIONAL ACTIVITIES

This story lends itself to all kinds of art and frieze work, as well as short pieces of drama.

1. Make lifesize cardboard model of Goliath, about 3 metres high, using aluminium foil as armour. Allow children to measure their heights against it.
2. Make David's equipment (rod, staff, knife, sling and five stones).
3. Dramatize story.
4. Sing: "Only a boy called David".

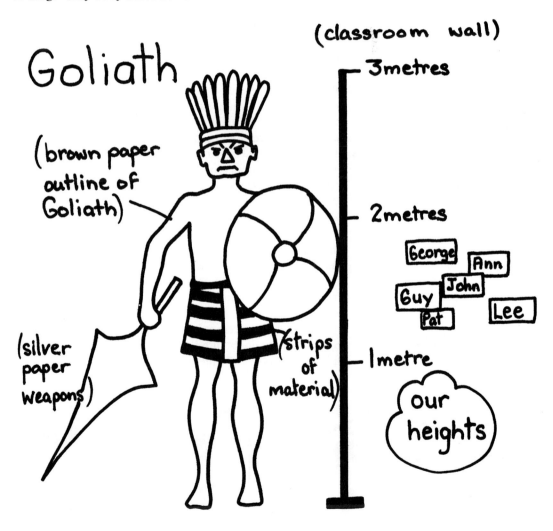

27

NAAMAN AND THE LITTLE MAID

2 Kings 5:1–15

AIM

1. To tell the story of Naaman and emphasize the necessity of obedience and simple trust.
2. Children will learn how a little girl, by her faith in God and willingness to talk about him, led a great commander to be healed.

INTRODUCTION

1. General discussion about what it is like to be away from home. Preparations and excitement before going on holiday.
2. Lead on to the story of how a young girl described as "a little maid" in 2 Kings 5:2, was *forced* to go far away from her home and family to live with people she had never seen before—Naaman, the great general, and his wife.

SUGGESTED PROCEDURE

1. Develop how she would still pray to God every morning and night as she had learned at home in Israel. Maybe she would remember how Joseph and Moses had been in strange lands and how they went on trusting in God and obeying him by being good and working hard.
2. Speak about her concern over Naaman's illness and discuss his nasty skin disease which made everyone afraid—so frightened that they wanted him to go away and live by himself.
3. Talk about how the little maid loved her mistress and did not like to see her so sad; her eagerness to tell her about God's servant, Elisha, who would be sure to help.
4. Naaman accepted the little girl's advice. Discuss the great preparations—taking silver and gold and ten suits of clothing—he was very wealthy and important.
5. What a stupid cure! The Jordan was such a narrow river compared with the beautiful rivers at home.
6. Emphasize how doubtful he was of obeying. Imagine how silly he felt dipping 1-2-3-4-5-6-7 times in the water. Then *clean*!

7. No wonder he wanted to tell everyone about how God had cured him. He must be a powerful and loving God. Naaman would always trust and obey God now.

8. Imagine how eagerly they awaited Naaman's return, the joy of the little girl on seeing her mistress no longer sad and her master cured.

9. Now it was just like her old home, the family praying to God and learning more about him.

OPTIONAL ACTIVITIES

1. Sing hymn of simple obedience, e.g. "Saviour teach me day by day", "The wise may bring their learning" (*The Church Hymnary*).

2. Drama: act out the story.
   Scene 1: Sadness of the family; the little girl speaks.
   Scene 2: Naaman meets Elisha—doubt—bathes seven times.
   Scene 3: Return and rejoicing. All say a "thank you" prayer to God.

3. Art: paint a picture on lines of the above drama. Children can choose to do one of the scenes or all three.

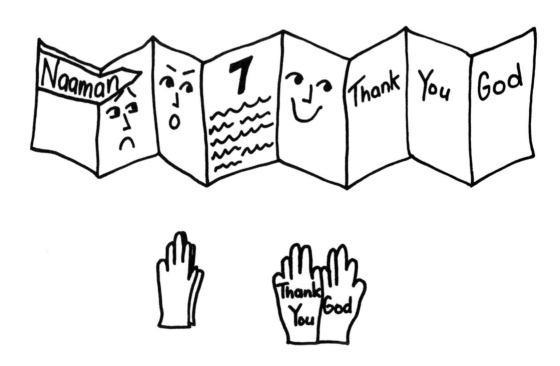

DANIEL IN THE LIONS' DEN

Daniel 6

AIM

To tell the story of Daniel and illustrate how he was protected and honoured because of his trust in God.

INTRODUCTION

Daniel was a prince brought up to trust in God. Israel was attacked by a foreign army and Jerusalem, the capital, was taken. Many people were taken prisoner and led off captive to this foreign country called Babylon. Daniel was one of these unfortunate people. Lead on to the main story of Chapter 6 but you may also wish to glance at Chapters 1 to 5 to get further background information.

SUGGESTED PROCEDURE

1. Discuss how Daniel might have felt being taken away to a foreign country without friends and family.
2. Tell how the king of the country, impressed by Daniel's appearance, decided to take Daniel to live in the palace, to teach him their language and to train him in leadership.
3. Explain how, despite all this, Daniel did not forget his own nationality nor did he forget the God that he worshipped. He prayed every day to Him and became a very popular person in the country.
4. When a new king called Darius came to the throne, he wanted to make Daniel Prime Minister since he was such a trustworthy person. Others were jealous and thought it wrong for a foreigner to hold such an important position so they plotted against him to try to find some fault that they could expose to the King. They found nothing wrong with anything he did. He worshipped his God but that was allowed . . . so far.
5. Daniel's enemies made up a plan to persuade the King that, since *he* was the greatest person on earth, there should be a law against anyone who worshipped a god instead of him. The King, pleased by such flattery, passed a law to this effect. The penalty for breaking it was to be thrown to the lions.
6. Describe how they spied on Daniel and reported to the King his daily praying to God. Sadly and reluctantly the King had to put the law into effect without favour to Daniel.
7. Graphically tell the story of Daniel's being put into the lions' den, his protection, the king's sleepless night and his morning visit to the den where he found Daniel unharmed, Daniel's release and pardon.

8 am

12 noon

9 pm

8. Tell how the law was changed and Daniel's God was recognized as the only true God. Stress the obedience and faithfulness of Daniel; stress also that God can protect us from danger.

OPTIONAL ACTIVITIES

1. Prayer: Lord, help us to trust you like Daniel, and to pray to you. Just as you protected Daniel from the lions you can help and guard us in danger if we trust in you.
2. Drama: The scenes could be set in different corners of the room.

   Corner 1: Enemies discussing Daniel, see him praying in Corner 2 and an evil plan forms in their minds.

   Corner 2: Daniel praying at his window.

   Corner 3: Delegation (from Corner 1) goes to the King with a proposition to proclaim a new law. The new law is proclaimed. After the proclamation, the enemies in Corner 1 see Daniel praying again and report to the King.

   Corner 4: Daniel put in lions' den.

   Next morning . . . etc. leading on to new decree.

colours: orange: yellow:
brown only
tissue paper + paint
black paper and glue for
bars.

curl paper
on scissor
blade

3. Collage: e.g. large lions, bars of den, Daniel in the middle.
4. Book: Make a concertina book with drawings of scenes from the story.
5. Sing: "Good Old Daniel", "Dare to be a Daniel".

Recipe for Dough

Life in Jesus' time

Water

camel's milk

goat's milk

olive oil

fish

eggs

quail

melons

pomegranates

lentils

olives

marrows

cucumbers

grapes

figs

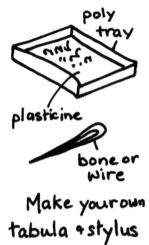

poly
tray

plasticine

bone or
wire

Make your own
tabula & stylus

Topic 2   School

We can safely assume that when Jesus was a boy, there was a school system throughout the country. Historians tell us that, at least one hundred years before the birth of Christ, a school was founded in Jerusalem. Although only from the humble home of a carpenter, Jesus would learn to read and write; He would be expected to know about the Law and the Prophets, the Bible of that time for the Jews. The churches, known as synagogues, were used as schools in the smaller towns and villages. In larger towns and cities there would be a separate building.

The pupils sat in a semi-circle round the rabbi or teacher, who was raised a little on a stool so that they could all see him. The alphabet was learned by constant repetition and they were expected to spend a lot of time on this at home. The pupils had a little wax tablet to write on. Each letter would then be written out by the teacher and put on a scroll. Once they had mastered the alphabet, reading was taught with the scriptures until many of the children knew long parts off by heart. The school day was very short since school closed between 10 am and 3 pm because of the heat. They probably started very early in the morning and would have a lot of work to learn at home for the next day.

At school they were taught that the Word of God had to become part of their life. To emphasize this point children were given interesting things to do as they learned. For example, the writing tablet it is believed was smeared with honey after they had written on it and they had to lick it off! Or they might be asked to eat small cakes which had passages of scripture written on them!

Topic 3   Clothes

What people wear depends on climate and how much they can afford to buy. Where Jesus lived it is warm and therefore the people in his time wore loose clothes to keep cool.

The poor wore simple clothes. Both men and women wore robes. A man's was generally white and came to his knees; a woman's was generally blue and reached her ankles. The women learned how to embroider the front of their robes with nice patterns, traditional to their particular village.

Round his waist the man wore a girdle made of leather or cloth and he kept money in a slit or pouch. When a man was working, the robe might get in his way so he would "gird up his loins", or tuck the lower part into the strap round his waist.

A cloak might also be worn; this was a heavy woollen cloth in dark and light brown stripes, sewn together with holes for the neck and arms. Only richer people wore this type but some servants borrowed them from their masters.

On their feet the poorer people wore simple sandals attached by thongs from the soles to their ankles. Many, however, went barefoot.

At night they had no special clothes for bed but simply loosened their clothes and lay down as they were.

I'm a poor villager

In the heat of the day something had to be worn on the head; the men wore turbans and the women wore a square piece of cloth which when folded shielded their eyes and protected their neck. It was held in place by a plaited cord.

The rich of course had more expensive clothes of cotton or silk and had coloured jackets or long-sleeved coats.

Often you would see a man with a little leather box strapped to his forehead and left arm. This was called a phylactery, which held pieces of parchment on which scripture was written. Only the very religious wore these, almost as a superstition.

You could often tell what a man did for a living by the clothes he wore. For example fishermen wore particular types of tunics and teachers had a blue fringe at the bottom of their coats.

Topic 4   Travel

Most roads were hard earth which became impassable in the wet season. Later the Romans built good roads but these were very few and only between main centres for easy movement of troops. They also put down milestones and built pavements.

The majority of people travelled by foot and, in case they were attacked by robbers, they went in groups. Goods were taken by ox cart or by donkey. Camels, of course, were used in sandy places and the very wealthy had chariots and horses.

Topic 5   Worship

Jesus was a Jew and Jews worshipped God. They met together on the seventh day of the week, known as the Sabbath, in a building called a synagogue (the Hebrew word for "meeting together" is *synago*) which everyone could see from a distance because of its height and position in the town. Women and children did not take part in the service but sat in a gallery above the main room. (You can read more about the form of service, etc. in the books listed in the Bibliography.)

Other topics to investigate: Crafts and Trades; Money; The Romans; The Temple; Jerusalem; Shepherds; The Weather; Plants and Animals in New Testament Times; Games and Pastimes; Fishing.

Bibliography

The following books were very useful when compiling these notes. Some are now out of print but reference to them in a library will allow the teacher to expand on the material given if desired.

Bible Stories Retold   Margaret McCrea   (Evans)
New Testament Stories Retold   Margaret McCrea   (Evans)
Life in New Testament Times   (Ladybird)

These other books would be of interest too.
Animals, Birds and Plants of the Bible   (Ladybird)
Children of The Bible   (Ladybird)
Jesus the Child   (Ladybird)
Buildings in the Bible   Ian Calvert   (Blackwell)
Crafts in the Bible   Ian Calvert   (Blackwell)
Farming in the Bible   Ian Calvert   (Blackwell)
Travel in the Bible   Ian Calvert   (Blackwell)

There are various sets of New Testament pictures, posters and filmstrips available.

THE CHRISTMAS STORY

INTRODUCTORY NOTE

Every year, when December comes round, teachers begin to prepare for Christmas with games, parties, decorations, etc. It is easy to enter this time with a sense of "old routine" and it is often difficult to tell the Story of Christmas in a fresh way. The story is always "new" to Infants and it helps if the teacher enters into the wonder and the excitement of the occasion.

Most of us do lessons on Christmas and it may be felt that to include detailed suggestions might be redundant; however the four lessons which follow will give the teacher some new ideas, it is hoped, and also emphasize the fact that the Christmas story must be viewed, not in isolation, but as part of a class programme in Religious Education for the session. Here are some points you may wish to consider when planning for Christmas:

1. Integrate the story with the daily life in the classroom (songs, craft, etc.).
2. Display books about Christmas and the Birth of Jesus as well as decorations.

coloured or white card circles...
sticky paper cut outs
or old Christmas cards...

Mobiles

God

sent

Jesus

3. As well as singing carols, listen to songs and carols on record or tape.
4. Take at least two weeks to cover these four lessons and prepare well beforehand.
5. We may think we know the Christmas story as told in the Bible but this time round, let us take out a modern version of the Bible and read it again.

BOOKS TO HELP YOU PLAN THE LESSONS

1. A modern version of the Bible, e.g. *Good News Bible*.
2. *Religious Education, Primary School Handbook* (Scottish Joint Committee on Religious Education), pages 32–6.
3. *Jesus is Born* (British and Foreign Bible Society).
4. *What Shepherds Saw, The Birth of Jesus, Strange New Star* (all Magic Picture Books by Scripture Union).
5. ''The Little Drummer Boy'' from *Seeing and Doing* Anthology of Poems and Songs (Thames Television).
6. *Come and Sing* (Scripture Union).
7. Poem ''How Far is it to Bethlehem?'' *Seeing and Doing* Anthology or *Book of a Thousand Poems*).
8. Slides and pictures, even up-to-date ones, showing fields and shepherds in the Holy Land, help to make the place and time of the story more of a reality.

AIM OF LESSONS

To tell the Christmas story in a meaningful way emphasizing the reasons for the celebrations and stressing ''giving'' more than ''getting'' as the true spirit of the season.

Lesson 1 Our Christmas

INTRODUCTION

Start off with the familiar. Ask pupils to draw what they would like for Christmas.

SUGGESTED PROCEDURE

1. What will generally emerge from the introduction is the "getting" aspect of the time: presents, parties, food. Try to introduce the idea that no one can receive unless someone else gives.
2. Talk about what their ideal Christmas might be. Discuss the plans, the excitement and the secrecy in choosing and giving presents, the making of decorations and giving cards for other people's pleasure as well as their own.
3. Discuss what it might mean to receive a gift of food if they were hungry, or clothes if they had only rags. It might be possible to relate this aspect to some tangible expression, e.g. making gifts for a children's or old folk's home or hospital. A tape of the class singing carols could be sent to a home or hospital.
4. Stress the point of 3. that the only thing given in return might be "thanks". Discuss what really nice gift they would like to give to a relative, even if they cannot afford it!
5. Talking about the secrecy aspect of presents, prepare the way for the next lesson by telling the children that God had a great gift that He was going to give to the world.

OPTIONAL ACTIVITIES

1. Prayer: Lord help us to enjoy giving as much as receiving.
2. Frieze: "parcel" with recipients names on it with the slogan "Christmas time is giving time".
3. Sing: "Hands to work and feet to run" (The Church Hymnary).

Lesson 2   The Greatest Gift of All

Matthew 1:18–25; Luke 2:1–7

INTRODUCTION

Recall the previous discussion about presents. Go on to tell about God's gift to the world.

brown paper stones

'God sent Jesus' into our world.

SUGGESTED PROCEDURE

1. Tell about God's promise to Mary that she would have a very special baby.
2. Go on to explain the reasons for the journey to Bethlehem; the difficulty in finding accommodation.
3. Let children talk about babies in cots and cradles in their homes and contrast with the manger where Jesus was born.
4. Do not overemphasize the hardships but stress the joy of the occasion for Mary and Joseph; the warmth of the straw and the swaddling clothes.

CONCLUSION

1. Sing: "A Christmas Secret" *(Come and Sing)*, as well as other carols.
2. Various art and craftwork.

Lesson 3   The Shepherds Hear of the Gift from God

Luke 2:8–20

INTRODUCTION

Talk about shepherds in Israel in Bible times.

SUGGESTED PROCEDURE

1. Tell the shepherds' story. Salient points are:
   (a) The scene on the hillside; shepherds looking after their sheep during the night.
   (b) A bright light appears in the sky—the shepherds are terrified.
   (c) The angel tells them not to be afraid, he was bringing good news.
   (d) The angel's message.
   (e) The choir of angels singing praises to God.
   (f) The shepherds go off to Bethlehem as they were told although they may have been surprised that a child of such importance should be born in a manger.
   (g) Their visit.
   (h) They return to their flocks praising God.
   (i) Talk about Jesus as God's gift for everyone, young and old, rich and poor.

nylon tights into ball shape

cone of stiff card

string

fur scraps

felt
white
brown
red
beige

piece of tweed

pipe cleaner

cut out template

stick on cotton wool

white card lightly coat with glue and sprinkle with glitter

lace

Joseph and Mary

Variations

feltpen decoration or sticky paper scraps

OPTIONAL ACTIVITIES

1. Prayer: "Lord we thank you for sending Jesus to this earth. Help us to remember at this time of year this special gift You gave to us."
2. Appropriate carols.

Lesson 4   The Star Which Told of God's Gift

Matthew 2:1–11

INTRODUCTION

Talk about the stars in the heavens, how they form patterns which man has used over the years to find his way. Some have called them God's guiding lights, especially before the modern day instruments were invented.

SUGGESTED PROCEDURE

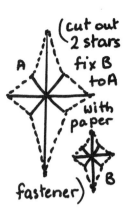

1. Tell the story stressing these points:
   (a) The wise men who studied the stars and got guidance and meaning from them.
   (b) Their wonder at the appearance of a new star; its movement across the sky; its significance (see verse 2).
   (c) The journey—including preparations and gifts for the King they hoped to meet.
   (d) The visit to Herod the King in Jerusalem in whose palace they expected a new king would be born. They are directed to Bethlehem.
   (e) Their further journey to Bethlehem following the star.
   (f) Arrival at Bethlehem and presenting of gifts.
2. Talk about how happy Mary and Joseph must have felt and how all these events would have confirmed that the baby Jesus was indeed very special.

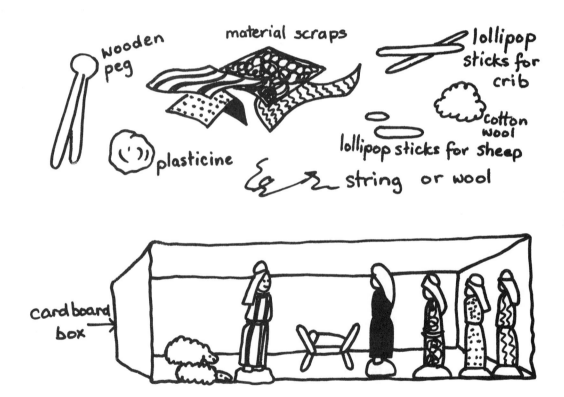

OPTIONAL ACTIVITIES

1. Prayer: "Thank you God for telling us about the wise men who were led to Jesus and who gave him gifts because he was a king. Show us what we can give him today and help us to love him too."
2. Songs: There are many songs about the Wise Men in carols and song books.
3. Poem: "How far is it to Bethlehem?" (*Book of a Thousand Poems* or *Seeing and Doing* Anthology).

4. Art:
   (a) Children can make a table decoration to take home.
   (b) A pomander is another easy gift for young children to make. They stick cloves into an orange (the more the better) and tie it with ribbon.
   (c) Other gifts can be made using the ideas shown.

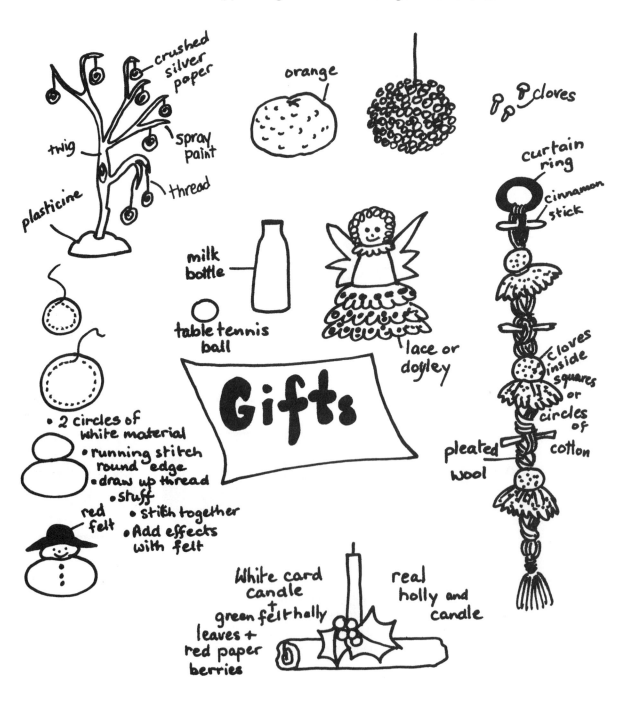

FRIENDS OF JESUS

The Boy Who Gave His Lunch to Jesus

Matthew 14:13–36; Mark 6:30–56; Luke 9:10–17; John 6:1–21

AIM

To illustrate the compassion of Jesus, in this case for the hungry, and the willingness of a boy to share with others.

INTRODUCTION

Discussion about packed lunches and picnics. What do the children like to take with them? Do they share it? Have they ever forgotten their lunch and been glad when someone shared theirs with them?

SUGGESTED PROCEDURE

1. Explain how Jesus had come away from the crowds to find some peace and quiet, but the people were not long in finding him, shattering all hopes of a peaceful day.
2. Give the boy in the story a name and an identity (e.g. Joachim a friend of the fishermen, etc.). The story could be told (on tape perhaps) in the first person. "My name is Joachim. One day . . . etc." Expand the story as told in the Bible from the boy's point of view.
   Stress the following main points imaginatively:
   (a) Packed lunch; barley loaves (like flat rolls); fish.
   (b) How much would his mother give him?
   (c) His outing round the Lake of Galilee, the crowds, Jesus healing, telling stories, etc.
   (d) He overhears the discussion about the crowd being hungry. Philip's contention, "Two hundred pennyworth of bread wouldn't be enough . . ." (several thousand pounds worth today perhaps).
   (e) The boy is hungry, should he keep it for himself or share it? He offers it to Andrew who gives it to Jesus.
   (f) Jesus shares the food; crowds seated in groups on the green grass; grace said; twelve baskets of left-over food.
   (g) He goes home to tell his mother about it.
3. Talk about sharing. Talk about saying grace before meals.

OPTIONAL ACTIVITIES

1. Model (paper or plasticine) of five loaves and two fish.
2. Wall display illustrating provision of food, harvest, etc., perhaps with graces underneath, e.g. "Thank you for the world so sweet".
3. Illustration of twelve baskets of food left over.
4. Oxfam, Save the Children Fund, etc., project and collection; send for information.

Fishermen Friends

John 1:35–42; Luke 5:1–11; Matthew 4:18–22; Mark 1:16–20

AIMS

1. To paint in the background to the gospel story.
2. To introduce the children to four of Jesus' friends.
3. To tell how Jesus first got to know these men (and they him), and subsequently called them to follow him.

INTRODUCTION

At least seven of Jesus' disciples were fishermen. This unit introduces us to four of them—the brothers Andrew and Peter, and their partners, James and John, also brothers.

By New Testament times there was a thriving fishing industry around the Sea of Galilee. Fish were usually caught by nets of which there were two kinds. One, still used in places, was a circular net with small weights attached to the edge. It was thrown with a spinning motion by someone standing on the shore and was designed to fall flat on the water. The weights would sink towards the bottom and the fisher would pull the cord and draw the net in with the fish trapped inside.

The other, a drag net, was larger with floats and weights attached to it. It was used from a boat and hung vertically in the water as it was dragged towards the boats or to shallow water, enclosing the fish in ever-decreasing circles. It could be used by one boat or by two in partnership.

mast – stick
sail – white cotton
boat – lollipop sticks
sea – string dipped in blue paint.

Brought to shore the fish had to be sorted before being sent to market. Some were eaten fresh while some were salted and dried for home consumption or for export.

On shore there was much to occupy the fishermen. Boats and sails had to be repaired; nets had to be cleaned and mended.

There were the usual satisfactions and disappointments of the fishing life. The Sea of Galilee is subject to sudden fierce squalls, a hazard at any time but especially so at night . . . and fishing was often done at night.

All this industry then—fishing, boat-building, fish-preserving, net-manufacture—is the background to the gospel story.

The suggestions that follow incorporate some conversations that are not recorded in the gospels but are of the kind that might well have taken place. Here they are simply a device for putting over information about events that *are* recorded—disappointing catches, storms, etc. Each lesson could with advantage occupy several days.

Lesson 1   Fishing on the Sea of Galilee

AIMS
1. To paint in the general scene.
2. To teach how drag-nets were used.

INTRODUCTION

Talk with the children about their visits to the seaside (or life by the sea if they are fortunate enough to live there).

If possible have on display pictures of fishing on the Sea of Galilee.

SUGGESTED PROCEDURE

Go on to discuss:

1. *The General Scene*

   Talk about the pictures in detail or describe what Jesus would see as he walked by the Lake—boats coming and going, fish being landed and sold, etc. It was an animated scene. Look out for similarities and differences between their own *experiences* and life in Galilee. (There's no need to describe fishing in this country except as experienced by them.)

2. *Fishing by Dragnet*

   Describe the net and how it was used. If possible have a piece of netting and give a demonstration with, of course, the help of the class. Failing that you might draw one.

3. *The Catch*

   Describe the landing, sorting, selling and use of the catch.

OPTIONAL ACTIVITIES
1. Throughout this unit have a display corner for the sea things brought in by the children.
2. Art: build up a collage as their knowledge increases.

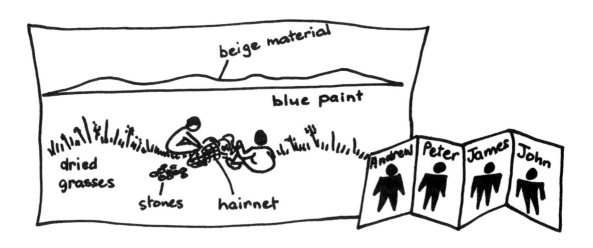

3. Speech and drama:
   (a) Be a fisherman, dragging nets to shore, etc. Work in partners or foursomes with impromptu conversation.
   (b) Sort the fish.
   (c) Be a merchant, buying fish for pickling.
   (d) Be a housewife buying at the market.
   These activities may be put together in sequence to form a playlet or may simply be done in twos or threes, each group acting out the situation of its choice.
4. Maths:
   (a) Shape: Give each child a kite shape and four or five triangles to assemble into a fish shape.
   (b) Sorting: Have paper fish of different sizes and colours for sorting activities. One colour might be inedible fish while others are edible, and so on.

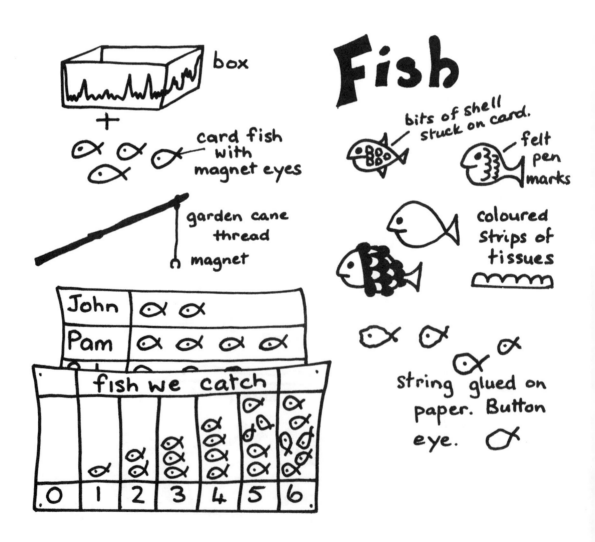

Lesson 2   Andrew and Peter

AIMS

1. To introduce Andrew and Peter.
2. To teach how nets are used.
3. To teach about the care of nets.

INTRODUCTION

Ask the children to describe fishing by dragnet.

SUGGESTED PROCEDURE

Tell about two fishermen Jesus had made friends with:

1. *Andrew and His Cast Net*

   One day walking by the sea, Jesus saw Andrew casting a net. He was using a different kind of net from that used in a boat. Describe it and how it is used.

2. *Peter Mending a Net*

   Further along, Jesus saw Andrew's brother Peter mending a net. He asked him if he had had a good catch. Yes, he had—so many that the net was torn with their weight; he described his fishing trip to Jesus. (Incorporate details from your own knowledge and imagination.) Now he was busy cleaning the nets and mending them. Some were already clean and drying on the rocks.

OPTIONAL ACTIVITIES

1. *Modelling*

   Make plasticine or pipe-cleaner fishermen mending and washing their nets. Nets can be made from the net bags in which fruit and vegetables are often sold.

2. *Music and Mime*

   Listen to Schubert's Piano Quintet in A Major (The Trout). Build up a mime routine to the music—casting nets, pulling in, emptying, salting, filling creels, washing nets, picking seaweed and shells out of them, mending and spreading them on the rocks to dry.

3. *Netting*

   Show the children basic netting stitches. Netting itself will be too difficult for them to do but they can appreciate the skill involved and they can imitate the arm movement.

   Show photographs of present-day fishermen mending nets as they sit on the beach with outstretched legs, their toes keeping the nets taut.

Lesson 3   James and John

AIMS

1. To introduce James and John.
2. To give some idea of the frustrations and dangers of the fishing life.

INTRODUCTION

Remind the children of the friends of Jesus they met in previous lessons.

SUGGESTED PROCEDURE

Tell how, another morning, Jesus came upon James and John with their father, Zebedee. They had several men working for them, all busy with the nets. They'd had a disappointing night, having caught no fish. They told Jesus how they had had to battle against a storm. Give as vivid a description as you can.

OPTIONAL ACTIVITIES

1. Do a finger-painting of a storm.
2. Have any of them experienced a storm at sea? Discussion.

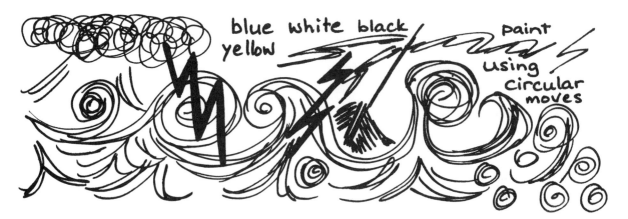

Lesson 4   Call of the Disciples

AIM

To tell how Jesus asked these four men to become disciples.

INTRODUCTION

Remind the children that now they know four of Jesus' friends. Do they remember their names? Talk about them.

SUGGESTED PROCEDURE

Tell the story of the calling of the disciples, emphasizing these points:

1. *Peter's Boat to the Rescue*
   Describe the crowds and the difficulty of addressing them. Jesus then recognized two boats and had an idea. (Can the children see how a boat might solve the difficulty?) Now all could hear and see Jesus.

2. *A Bumper Catch of Fish*

Jesus suggested they go and let the nets down. Simon demurred;
"We've been out all night and caught nothing. Nevertheless . . ."
They caught so many fish that there were too many for their net and
they had to call James and John to their aid. So with both ships full,
they came to land. What a catch! They were absolutely astonished.

3. *The Call of the Disciples*

Jesus told Peter that he had new work for him and then invited all
four of them to leave their fishing and come with him. He said, "You
won't be catching fish any more. From now on you will catch people. I
will make you fishers of men". From then on they would be helping
Jesus in his work of teaching and healing. They left their work in good
hands. (Zebedee had helpers, they should remember.) They went with
Jesus.

OPTIONAL ACTIVITIES

1. Writing: In their best writing the children copy:

> I will make you fishers of men
>
> ANDREW   JAMES
>
> PETER   JOHN

They could write on card and decorate the edge with sea symbols.

2. Language: Read some poems about fish and fishing.

Read Psalm 107:23–31, in either a prose or metrical version.

This unit might form part of a project on the sea or on fishing. In that case
a comparison with fishing at home could be made in some detail.

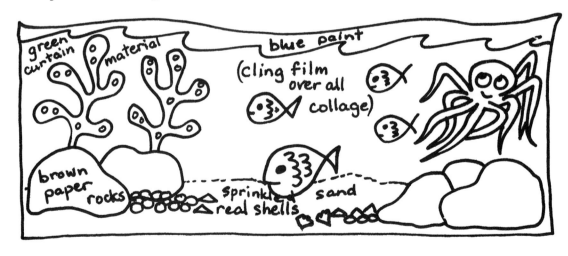

Zacchaeus in the Sycamore Tree

Luke 19:1–10

AIM

To illustrate the change which meeting Jesus had on the life of Zacchaeus.

INTRODUCTION

Discuss how sometimes children can be unpopular with others. Lead on to the story of Zacchaeus who was unpopular.

SUGGESTED PROCEDURE

1. Tell why Zacchaeus was a rich man; he was a tax collector for the Romans, unpopular at any time but even more so because he took more than he ought.
2. A great event was going to take place in his home town; there was to be a special visitor and everyone wanted to see him and speak to him. Talk about what happens when there is a visit by some well-known person to a place, the jostling for a space, etc. Jesus was coming to Jericho and Zacchaeus wanted to see him especially.
3. As he was so unpopular, no one would make a space for him, and he was small so he had to find a secret vantage point. He climbed up into a wide spreading sycamore tree, and waited for Jesus to pass by.
4. Imagine his surprise when Jesus stopped to speak right under his tree! What more could he want? Again, imagine his surprise when Jesus spoke to him in front of all the people and said that he was going to visit him in his house.
5. Discuss the shock and surprise of the crowd as Jesus went off with this "friend of the Romans". Discuss what Zacchaeus must have felt like when Jesus spoke to him so kindly.
6. After a talk with Jesus, Zacchaeus offered his life to him as a disciple and promised to give half his goods to the poor and four times as much back as he had stolen from people. Zacchaeus now had the best friend in the world. Jesus is like that today—ready to be everyone's friend and to help them.
7. Talk about the reaction of the neighbours and friends to this change in Zacchaeus' life.

OPTIONAL ACTIVITIES

1. Prayer: We thank you Lord Jesus that you always care for us and are willing to be our friend.
2. Act out the story or make a tape of Zacchaeus telling his story.
3. Draw or paint the scene or make a collage.

lonely

4. Action Song (to the tune of "Old King Cole")

> Zacchaeus was a very little man,
> A very little man was he,
> He climbed into a sycamore tree
> For he wanted the Lord to see
> For he wanted the Lord to see.
>
> And as the Saviour passed that way,
> He looked up to the tree.
> "Zacchaeus", he said, "Will you come down,
> For I'm coming to your house for tea,
> Oh yes! I'm coming to *YOUR* house for tea".
>
> Anon.

STORIES JESUS TOLD

The Lost Sheep

Luke 15:3–7

AIM

To show the care that God has for us as individuals.

INTRODUCTION

Talk about being lost. Ask children to recount experiences of being lost or separated from their parents in a crowd. How did they feel? Who found them? etc.

SUGGESTED PROCEDURE

This story is given in very little detail in the Bible. It is suggested that you expand the story stressing these main points:

1. The good relationship which the shepherd had with his sheep; he would know them individually.
2. His constant care for them.
3. His distress if even one is harmed or lost.
4. His unfailing concern as he searches.
5. His joy when he finds the one which is lost.

wooden spoon

felt pen features

fur fabric

material scraps

fold made of stones... plasticine or dough

the story of the lost 🐑

danger

safe

tray

You can make up a scene for the incident yourself, basing it on expanded versions already written for children. For those who do not have access to any of these the following example could be read or used as a basis for telling the story in your own words.

Story

One day Jesus told a story about a sheep that got lost. It lived with the rest of the sheep in a large flock cared for by a kind shepherd. This shepherd spent a lot of time looking after his sheep and guarding them night and day from wild animals and other dangers in this wild open country. At night, when he put them into a fold he used to sleep across the entrance; in fact, he was the "door" and nothing could get in without going over the top of him. (You could expand on the customs of shepherds in Bible times.) In these days the shepherd didn't drive his sheep with dogs, but he would walk ahead of them and lead them to the good pastures and to water.

Walking ahead of them one day he was leading them to some nice juicy grassland and to a stream where they could drink. They all followed him but one little sheep was enjoying the grass so much that he didn't follow the others when they went on to have a drink of water in the pool. When he lifted his head, they had just gone round a rocky area and he didn't see where they had gone. He panicked and went round in circles before running off in the opposite direction. He wandered on and on, getting more and more lost as he did so, until he started out on a path which the shepherd always avoided because it was dangerous. Suddenly, without warning, he fell into a deep hole in the ground. He struggled to get out until he was so tired that he fell down and tried to cry out hoping that some-one would find him before some wild animal found him and attacked him. In the meantime, the shepherd did not realize that one of his sheep had wandered off. It was sometime later, when he was gathering them together to return to the fold, that he realized that there was one missing; he had to find it before it got dark. He searched and searched over the dangerous paths until at last he found it. Putting the sheep over his shoulder he found his way back to the fold. At the end of the day he was very very tired but very happy that he had found his lost sheep.

OPTIONAL ACTIVITIES

1. Talk about Jesus, his care for us and how he is concerned about everything we do.
2. Talk about trust in God as our guide and helper. A prayer on this theme may be appropriate.
3. Choose hymns and choruses about Jesus as the Shepherd.
4. Art or dramatic activities could portray the story.
   (a) The Lost Sheep.
   (b) The Worried Shepherd.
   (c) Found at Last!

The Lost Coin

Luke 15:8–10

AIM

To remind children how happy they are to find something they had lost and to show them that God loves us and wants us close to Him. To familiarize children with Jesus' land.

INTRODUCTION

Read the story carefully. Know the background—the coin had sentimental value as part of a head-dress given as a wedding present by her husband. Houses were very dark, with only one window. The floor was covered with rushes which were swept out daily.

coins sewn on
roll of material

SUGGESTED PROCEDURE

1. Discuss with children how they feel when they lose something they are fond of. What do they do? How good it is to find it.
2. Jesus told a story of a lady who lost something very precious. It was a coin from the lovely headband her husband gave her when they got married. Where does your mother wear her wedding ring?
3. "It must be in the house," she thought. She got her brush, and swept her floor very carefully, examining the rushes and listening for a clink. There was no coin! She counted the coins on the band again—1, 2, 3, 4, 5, 6, 7, 8, 9, yes, one was missing. Now she lit a lamp and looked in the corners, and at last, away in a very dark corner, far from the one small window, there it was!
4. Out she ran and told all her neighbours about what had happened and how happy she now was.
5. Jesus tells us that God loves us even more than the lady loved her coin. He also tells us that God is very happy when we love Him and try to be like Him.

OPTIONAL ACTIVITIES

1. Prayer: Dear Father, thank you for loving me and caring for me. Please help me to love you too.
2. Draw a sad face with a head-dress of nine coins.
   Draw a coin, a lamp, a brush.
   Draw a happy face with a head-dress of ten coins.
3. Drama: four scenes
   The loss—the brushing and the lamp, peering into the corners—found!—telling the neighbours.
4. Sing: "God, who made the earth" (The Church Hymnary).

The Good Samaritan

Luke 10:25–37

AIM

To tell the story simply as a story Jesus told to the people around him. To remind children that it is not only good to help people who are hurt or sad, but it makes God happy when we do this.

INTRODUCTION

Know the details of the story thoroughly. Use the following background information sparingly as the story develops. A lawyer was an interpreter of Jewish Scripture—our Old Testament. (Omit him with young pupils or just call him a clever man.) A priest was allowed to officiate at the Temple, a high honour, only twice a year. A Levite was a Temple singer. If either touched a dead body they would be unclean and would lose their chance of taking part in the Temple worship, so they were taking no chances. Samaritans were not pure Jews and were despised by all Jews. The road was very very steep and dangerous and robberies were common.

SUGGESTED PROCEDURE

1. Discuss with children times when they were hurt or unhappy. Who usually comes and helps? Parents? Family? Friends? Teachers? Neighbours?

2. Have you ever been helped by a stranger? Someone who helped you up when you had fallen off your bike, for example? Someone who gave you a hankie to wipe your tears or clean your knees? Someone who got your ball or your boat back when it had drifted away on the water?

3. Jesus likes people to do this sort of thing—help people who are hurt or unhappy—not just our friends, but strangers too. He told this story to show us what he means.

4. Tell how in Jesus' time, when people went on journeys they either rode a donkey or walked beside a donkey which carried their luggage—or, simply walked.

   One day a man was walking up a very, very steep road to a big city, called Jerusalem, when robbers attacked him and not only stole his money, but also stole his clothes and hit him very hard. They left him lying on the rough road, all cut and miserable.

   Along came a priest—good, he will help—no, he passed by on the other side.

   Along came a singer called a Levite—surely he will help—no, he too went by on the other side.

   Maybe they were in a hurry, or did not want to get dirty, or were afraid the robbers might come back and hurt them. (With first Infants just call them important men.) Poor man, what will happen to him?

   Now along came a man from another land—a Samaritan. (Ask the children to say that name two or three times.) He was a total stranger but he came over and felt very sorry for the poor dirty and unhappy man, lying on the ground. He bathed his cuts, put on bandages, helped him on to his donkey and took him to an inn. In Bible times this was merely a shelter without any other services. The Samaritan had to give the innkeeper a lot of money so that he would fetch and carry, supply warm coverings, bring water, change bandages and cook for the traveller until he was well again.

5. When Jesus told this story he asked who was the good and kind person. What do you think the people said? Of course, but Jesus added something else, he said, "Go and do as he did". He tells us the same today.

Very briefly get examples from class of being "Good Samaritans". Maybe we should say a prayer asking God to help us—"Dear Father, we thank you for Jesus' stories. Make us like the Good Samaritan, kind to all, even people who are strangers".

OPTIONAL ACTIVITIES
1. The story lends itself easily to drama.
    (a) The traveller on his own.
    (b) The robbery—not too rough or realistic.
    (c) The priest—passes by.
    (d) The Levite—passes by.
    (e) The Samaritan's kind action.
    (f) At the inn.
2. In art, each child can draw a kind deed and these can be mounted on a
    frieze.
3. Sing: "Jesus' hands were kind hands" *(The Church Hymnary)*.

PEOPLE JESUS HELPED

Jesus Heals a Little Girl

Mark 5:22–4, 35–43

AIM

To tell the story of Jairus's daughter.

INTRODUCTION

Discuss with children times when they have been ill and their parents have had to send for the doctor.

SUGGESTED PROCEDURE

1. The teacher should first become familiar with the details of the story of Jairus and his daughter. This man was a well-known person in the area who would be able to afford all the best doctors.
2. Discuss his despair when his daughter seemed to be getting worse each day instead of better. However he heard of Jesus healing others and, although he was an important person, he went himself to ask Jesus to come and heal his daughter.
3. When Jesus reached the house, a great crowd of people were crying outside because it was assumed that she had died, but Jesus said, "She is not dead—she is only sleeping." He sent all the mourners away. He took three of his close friends and the girl's parents and went to her bedside. Taking her hand, Jesus said, "Little girl, it is time to get up". Jesus told her mother to give her something to eat so she hurried off to make a meal.

OPTIONAL ACTIVITIES

1. See lesson on "Hands" at the end of this series. Ideas could be adapted for this.
2. Sing "Jesus' hands were kind hands" *(The Church Hymnary)*.
3. Art:
   (a) Craft activities can include making a model of the house and people, bed, etc. as if it were a stage setting.
   (b) Make a "From sadness to joy" frieze.
   (c) Make "Get Well Soon" cards for anyone you know who is ill.
   (d) Draw people who help us.

Shoe box

old saucer covered with papier mâché

pipe cleaners

paper face

Look inside the house!

+ scrap material tied on head and body

Get Well

Get Well

Get Well

Get Well

Blind Bartimaeus

Mark 10:46–52

AIM

To tell how Jesus helped a blind man to see.

INTRODUCTION

Discuss blindness briefly, the problems, etc.

SUGGESTED PROCEDURE

1. One day Jesus and his disciples were making their way to Jerusalem, via Jericho, a fifteen mile walk. Jericho was the last stopping place for the pilgrims making their way to the Holy City and on that road it was common for beggars to sit at the roadside. Explain who the beggars were (mostly disabled people who couldn't work).
2. Bartimaeus had been a beggar for a long time; he was blind and could do no work. His hearing being very acute he heard a crowd of people approaching and asked what it was all about. Someone mentioned that Jesus of Nazareth was coming that way; Bartimaeus, who would normally talk to passers-by, had heard of this man who did good and had heard too that he touched people and healed them.
3. Ask children what they think the blind man would do when Jesus passed by. When he shouted out to attract Jesus' attention, the people round about him told him to be quiet. Bartimaeus shouted even more loudly until Jesus stopped and asked for him.
4. Go on to tell that Jesus made him see and he was able to join the crowd following Jesus up the road.

OPTIONAL ACTIVITIES

1. Prayer: Lord we thank you for making Bartimaeus see. Be with all those who are ill and bless them too.
2. The theme of blindness could be developed generally, referring to the help that blind people get today; braille, guide dogs, talking books, etc.
3. The healing aspect, developed in the prayer, could be extended to consider the skills and dedication of those who care for the blind and partially sighted.
4. Make a book of beautiful things that Bartimaeus would enjoy seeing for the first time.

feelie box

cotton squares containing dried peas beans stones cornflakes etc.

picture drawn with candle

What will happen?

paint over with blue paint

what helps me?

braille
guide dog
white stick
sounds
friends

a blind person

this is what you see

feel

The Storm at Sea

Mark 4:35–41; Matthew 8:23–7; Luke 8:22–5

AIM

To tell how Jesus used his power to calm the stormy sea and comfort his disciples.

INTRODUCTION

Using a picture of a ship at sea, talk about the dangers of a storm. Discuss personal experiences when children were afraid of the sea.

SUGGESTED PROCEDURE

1. Having read the account yourself, tell it vividly to the class. The main points might be:
   (a) Explanation about "Sea of Galilee"; not a sea, but a large lake which was often stormy and dangerous when the wind was in a certain direction.
   (b) A direct way of getting to the other side of the lake, especially when Jesus was very tired.
   (c) Jesus fell asleep; storm arose and they were all afraid, although some of them were fishermen used to the sea.
   (d) They wakened Jesus who asked why they were frightened. He spoke to the wind and waves which became calm. They were still frightened when they realized he could control the wind and the waves.
   (e) They reached the other side safely.
2. Discuss Jesus' interest in our feelings in all situations. The story makes the point that we should remember to trust him. When God is with us he can help us to be calm and brave in difficult times.

OPTIONAL ACTIVITIES

1. Prayer: Thank you God, for being with us when we need you. Help us to trust you even when we are afraid.
2. Discuss the dangers that can arise at sea with fishermen and sailors, especially those who risk their lives to bring food to us. This might be linked to an environmental study of the sea.
3. The scene could be drawn or painted or retold in dramatic form with pupils taking part.
4. Sing: "God is always near me" (*The Church Hymnary*).

storm picture paint

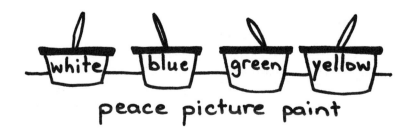

peace picture paint

THE EASTER STORY

Easter

AIM

To teach the Easter story and:
1. The appreciation of the beauty of Spring and the concept of "New Life" will be enriched.
2. Children will learn the simple facts of the last week of Jesus' earthly life.
3. Children will, through story and song, appreciate that Jesus is still alive and with us today.

INTRODUCTION
1. The classroom should be bright with a Spring frieze "New Life in Spring" depicting flowers, buds and trees, birds, lambs, fluffy chicks, etc. The nature table should be in evidence and bulbs on display.

2. The teaching must emphasize Easter joy (not the cruelty of the Cross) and the keynote is "Jesus Is Risen". It is enough to say that some people did not like Jesus and wanted to kill him. Finally they did this and his friends thought they would never see him again. Then they received a wonderful surprise—he came back to them and seemed nearer than before. One way of putting this, is that instead of being in one place at one time, he is now everywhere all the time. Jesus died but he now lives a new life.

3. Briefly the events of Holy Week are:

Sunday	Triumphal Entry. Mark 11:1–10; Matthew 21:1–11. Though Hosanna means "save us we beseech you" Psalm 118:25, it can simply be a shout of joy, "Hooray".
Monday	Cleansing the Temple. Mark 11:15–19; Matthew 21:12–22.
Tuesday	Questions in the Temple. Mark 12.
Wednesday	Anointing at Bethany. Matthew 26:1–13.
Thursday	The Last Supper The Arrest in the Garden of Gethsemane
Friday	The Crucifixion
Sunday	The Resurrection. Because Jesus rose on Sunday, Christians changed their holy day from the old Jewish Sabbath on Saturday to a Sunday.

FORMAT

Ideas but not binding:

1. Song.
2. Discussion centred on picture or frieze.
3. Story with reference to Bible.
4. Song.
5. Prayer.
6. Activity.

Several of these lessons may take more than one period of time if art or drama is included.

PREPARATION

1. In preparation children might learn some or all of these hymns—one or two verses should suffice:
   "God who made the earth", "There is a green hill", "Jesus Christ is risen today", "Hosanna, loud hosanna", "Children of Jerusalem" (all from *The Church Hymnary*).
2. It is assumed a Spring frieze and nature table will be in evidence.

MAKING AN EASTER GARDEN

1. Use a sand tray, table top or other large surface.
2. Put in sufficient earth to allow seeds to grow and plant quick-growing ones like mustard and cress.
   or
   If above is not possible paint a sheet of cardboard, or polystyrene, green and lay seed trays and flowers in plastic tubs on this.
3. Mount your Spring flowers and leafy twigs in earth.
4. In centre build a hill of polystyrene or similar material and paint it brown or beige or grey.
5. Make woolly lambs from cottonwool, etc. to go at foot of hill. (Children will probably add rabbits and chicks.)

card..
cotton
wool..
sticks..

Argus poster with trees

hyacinth

buds

green or yellow cloth

New life comes again

Lesson 1   New Life in God's World

AIM

To increase children's awareness of the joy and beauty of new life in
Spring.

Children will be prepared for the element of joy in the Easter story.

SUGGESTED PROCEDURE

1. Sing: "God who made the earth".
2. Read Song of Solomon 2:11–12. People in Bible times also enjoyed
   this time.
3. Examine some of the lovely things on the frieze or nature table—
   lambs, chicks, flowers, trees, birds, etc.

   Have two clearly contrasting pictures, one a cold dead winter scene,
   the other a bright spring one.

   Notice: Grey skies are blue.
   Snowy ground is now green.
   Black and brown trees have green leaves.
   Brown earth has now bright flowers.
   Birds are flying; lambs, rabbits, chickens are running about.

   What looked so dull is now full of life.

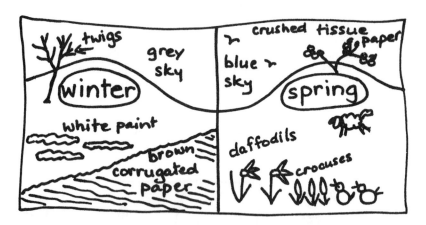

4. Sing: "Stand up, Clap hands", or "Morning has broken" (from *Someone's Singing, Lord* or Ladybird *Hymns and Songs*).
5. Mime: (a) Sit curled up on a chair.
   (b) Legs go down to be roots.
   (c) Arms go up like shoots.
   (d) Spread out hands like leaves opening.
   (e) Faces like flowers smile at the sun.
6. Prayer: "We thank you loving Father for all lovely things in Spring", or
   use Ladybird prayers page 14 or 16 from *Book of Prayers*.
7. Make an Easter garden. See notes. Spare "lambs", etc. can go on the
   frieze already on wall.

   The element of thanking God must not be lost as we prepare for the
   last verse "God, who sent His Son to die on Calvary" from the hymn
   "God, who made the earth."

everyone

is

happy

Lesson 2   The Triumphal Entry

Matthew 21 : 1–11

AIM

To show how Jesus entered Jerusalem on a donkey as a *king*.
Children will, through drama, music and art, experience the idea of praising Jesus the King.

SUGGESTED PROCEDURE

Palm Branches...

green sugar paper...

fold in half..

cut from side to fold..

glue stick up centre fold for strength.

1. Sing: "Children of Jerusalem".
2. Why do we sing this hymn? It reminds us of a time when children sang while Jesus rode by them on a donkey to Jerusalem. Tell the story from Mark 11 ; 1–10 and read parts from a modern version of the Bible, e.g. *Good News Bible*. Talk about the children gathering to watch pilgrims going to Jerusalem for the Feast of the Passover (just say a special occasion!) and how excited they were to see Jesus and his disciples. They just couldn't help cheering as he passed.
3. Organize children to enact the scene:
   (a) Use your dressing-up box for the central figure of Jesus and two or three of his disciples. A broom will do for the donkey.
   (b) Have leafy branches ready—the real thing is better than paper ones. Tie up with "Signs of Spring" lessons.
   (c) While some perform the scene, no one will be left out as all can sing "Hosanna, loud hosanna". (Verse 1 will do, or one or more verses can be learned if class is able.) Have a second or third performance if all want to take part.
4. Prayer: Father we thank you for Jesus our King who rode into Jerusalem on a donkey. We are glad that children sang to him and waved their palm branches. We thank you that we can still sing to Jesus and praise him.
5. Consolidate the lesson by making a big frieze entitled 'Jesus Is Our King". Each child (and the teacher) draws him/herself and mounts this round the central figure of Jesus on the donkey. The teacher can either paint the central figure or do the outline and children can fill in the bodies with scraps of material or paper tissue, etc.

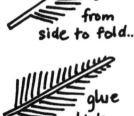

donkey....

old broom handle...

... Padded cushion..

card. board .ears...

brown blanket or curtain....

..felt features...

Lesson 3   The Last Supper

Mark 14:22–6

AIM

To establish that Jesus promised never to leave his friends.
Children will learn about the Last Supper and the Garden, and Jesus' promise not to leave his friends.

SUGGESTED PROCEDURE

1. Sing again "Children of Jerusalem" or "Hosanna, loud hosanna", to remind children of the last lesson.
2. Later that week Jesus had a very special meal with his friends. Show children a picture of a family at table, e.g. Frances Hook's *Present Day Pictures* and talk about eating with family and friends, see Ladybird *Hymns and Songs*, page 19. Jesus had a meal like this with his twelve close friends or disciples. Show a picture from a modern set of New Testament ones to depict the Last Supper. A Last Supper picture can be made also. (If desired this can be a follow-up activity or preparatory activity—the teacher draws a table and children can paint pictures of Jesus and the twelve disciples; bread and cups to go round and on it.) Discuss what people ate at meals in Jesus' time—fruit, lamb, bread, wine. We remember especially the joy of eating together with friends.
3. Before they ate, Jesus would say "grace"—let the children sing or say their favourite grace. The disciples would sit together and because this was a special feast, as well as eating and drinking, they would sing Old Testament psalms, e.g. "Give thanks to the Lord for He is Good". Children could sing "God is always near me". Jesus also said he would always be with us. He would never leave his friends. They were all very happy together.
4. Prayer: We thank you Lord Jesus for telling us you will always be among us. Bless our fun and parties, our work and our play.
5. As it was very hot in the room they all went out together to a Garden, called Gethsemane. Focus attention on the Easter Garden now.
6. Either do the class picture of Jesus and his friends at supper (or in the garden) or draw own pictures.

Lesson 4 Arrest, Crucifixion and Resurrection of Jesus

Mark 14:32–52; Mark 15; John 20:1–18
(These readings are for teacher's reference—only John 20 concerns the children.)

AIM

To teach simply the story of Jesus being killed and rising again.
Children will learn the simple fact that Jesus had enemies who killed him. They will absorb the joy of "Jesus is risen".

SUGGESTED PROCEDURE

1. Sing "God who made the earth". Sing last verse very quietly.
2. Remind children of the Supper and the Garden. Explain that Jesus had many friends because of the good things he said and did (ask for examples briefly). But he also had enemies who were jealous because so many people loved Jesus and followed him. These people wanted him killed so they sent soldiers into the Garden to capture him. They took Jesus away and his disciples were very frightened.
3. We have just sung a lovely hymn about the things God made. Now we will think of the last verse, how Jesus died and rose up to life again.
   The soldiers took Jesus to a hill called Calvary where he died on a cross. (Make sure Easter Garden is in a central position.) The disciples and Jesus' mother and the women who followed Jesus were very sad. They thought they would never see Jesus' kind face again or hear his voice or watch him helping people.
   Sing "There is a green hill". All the rest of Friday and Saturday the friends of Jesus stayed together, frightened and sad. Now tell the story of Easter Sunday morning from John 20:1–18 as simply and graphically as possible. Use the Easter Garden to show how Jesus appeared again to his friends.
   Stress that all fears and tears are gone. Jesus was alive again and was keeping his promise never to leave his friends.
4. Prayer: We thank you Jesus, that you rose from the tomb and are alive with us now and forever.
5. Sing "Jesus Christ is risen today". Select one or two verses if class is very young or immature.
6. Paint and roll Easter eggs (hard-boiled and brought by the children). Explain that rolling them represents the stone rolling away.
   Make Easter cards to send to friends, especially lonely or sick people.

build
`Jerusalem`
on table...
Surround with
'wall' of card from
boxes...
houses of cereal,
food packets...
Cover with offwhite
paper or paint.
roof of marg. carton
Build hills of
moss outside
walls... plant tiny
flowers....
crosses of twigs...
a stone ....

biscuit tin lid
plants
&
stones

Lesson 5   The Easter Service in the Classroom

AIM

To consolidate previous work and to evoke the joy of Easter.

SUGGESTED PROCEDURE

1. At Easter we remember that Jesus died and rose again. Look at the walls to remind us of Springtime.
2. Look at the "Triumphal Entry" picture. Sing a verse of "Hosanna, loud hosanna". What does this picture tell us? Discuss.
3. Look at the Last Supper picture. What did Jesus promise his friends during his meal with them? Never to leave them. But what happened after they went into the Garden? Focus attention on the Garden and recapitulate that Jesus was killed and his friends were sad. Consolidate with verses from "There is a green hill".
4. But we know he rose again. Read a verse or two from John 20:1–18. Sing "Jesus Christ is risen today".
5. Prayer: We thank you again for Easter. Help us to have bright happy faces when we remember that Jesus is alive and with us.
6. Either write greetings on Easter cards to give to people or make these if not already done so, or make another card to mount on a classroom "Jesus Is Alive" frieze.

● start off with coloured card....
  draw shapes of rabbit, flower or egg or leave plain...
  use felt pens or sticky paper for decor....

cotton egg cosy

yoghurt carton

eggs...

GENERAL TOPIC

HANDS

This is an example of a general theme which teachers can integrate into a Religious Education programme, linked perhaps with an Environmental Study. Each lesson may take up more than one day.

AIMS

To help the children to appreciate their hands and to encourage a sense of responsibility in their use.

To increase their awareness and appreciation of the skills and concern of people who contribute to their well-being, e.g. parents, teachers, nurses.

To evoke a response of gratitude to their Creator and to help them realize with the psalmist that they are "wonderfully made".

Throughout the project have a display of people using their hands in a variety of ways. Children will doubtless bring pictures as the work proceeds.

Lesson 1   Speaking Hands

Matthew 19:13–15; Mark 10:13–16; Luke 18:15–17.

AIMS

To consider our hands as a means of communication.

To tell the story of Jesus blessing the children and to help the class understand that Jesus welcomes children now as warmly as he did then.

INTRODUCTION

Say, "I'm going to speak to you with my hands. Watch". Beckon to a child to come to you and ask the children what you are saying. Go on to "say" other things with your hands while they translate into words. There are, of course, limits to what can be communicated thus but try some of these:

(a) Don't do that again! *(wagging a finger)*

(b) Look! *(pointing)*

(c) I like that. *(clapping)*

(d) I'm angry. *(shaking fist)*

(e) Sh! *(finger to mouth)*

(f) I'm scared. *(wringing hands)*

(g) Goodbye! *(waving)*

Alternatively you might speak while they make appropriate gestures.

SUGGESTED PROCEDURE

1. Go on to discuss examples of speaking hands. Some topics are:

   (a) *Deaf-and-dumb alphabet.* Show them it. Some might learn to spell their own name in it.

   (b) *Conducting music.* They can talk about your gestures as you conduct their music-making. Let them take turns conducting the class. Play some music and let them all beat time to it.

   (c) *Customs:* shaking hands; saluting; clapping at a concert ("I like that"); praying hands.

2. Tell the story of Jesus and the children, perhaps through the eyes of one of the children or of a mother.

   (a) Children brought to Jesus so that he might touch them.

   (b) The disciples send the parents away—possibly because they thought Jesus was too busy to be bothered with mere children.

   (c) Jesus' response. He called them to him and said, "Let the little children come to me", as he took them in his arms. Do they know what he did then? He laid his hands on them and blessed them. What were Jesus' hands saying?

   They were saying, "You are welcome to come to me. I want you to be happy. I love you". That's the kind of person Jesus is.

OPTIONAL ACTIVITIES

1. Art:
    (a) Wall panel. Children paint their hands and make a print on a background paper. Either have the paper of such size that there is no overlapping of prints, or restrict the size and the range of colour (to two or three) so that there is quite a lot of overlapping.

    (b) Give each child a piece of paper about 25 cm by 20 cm. He spreads out each hand at any angle and draws the outline. He divides the hand arbitrarily into several parts and, using one colour only, fills in each area in different ways (lines, dots, solid colour, etc.).

The pages are then joined together to form a panel.

2. Speech: Learn some poems with finger-play;
    e.g. "Incey, wincy spider."

    or Shut them, open;
        Shut them, open;
        Shut them, open;
        Clap, clap, clap!

        Shut them, open;
        Shut them, open;
        Lay them in your lap!

    or *(Holding hands up, palms facing and apart)*
        These birds are sleepy. *(Left hand droops)*
        These birds are tired today. *(Right hand droops)*
        Tomorrow they will spread their wings,
        And flutter far away. *(Fingers flutter as arms are spread out and round and brought back to rest behind their backs.)*

3. Sing: "In Galilee beside the sea"; "I am so glad that Jesus said" (both from *Come and Sing*); "Jesus loves the little children" (*C.S.S.M. Choruses*); "Jesus loves me, this I know (*The Church Hymnary*).

Lesson 2   Working Hands

AIMS

1. To foster a respect for the skills of others.
2. To encourage a legitimate pride in work well done.
3. To contribute towards the building-up of a picture of the home life of Jesus.

INTRODUCTION

Refer to your wall display and discuss the examples of working hands.

SUGGESTED PROCEDURE

1. *Play a Game*

   Mime some familiar activities and ask the children what you are doing, e.g.

   (a) Playing the piano,
   (b) Painting a door,
   (c) Drinking tea,
   (d) Washing hands and face.

   Variations of this can follow, e.g. children miming while others guess. They can show how their parents use their hands at home.

2. *Their Homes*

   Lead on to a discussion of their parents' work and of how, through it, they show their love and care for their children.

   Talk about how they help their parents. Do they enjoy watching them making something—a cake, do-it-yourself job, etc.? (Most young children really enjoy working with their mother or father, feeling they're actually making a contribution.) Stress the feeling of companion-ship, of shared pleasure.

3. *Jesus' Home*

   Tell them how Jesus as a boy watched Joseph at work and learned to use the various tools in the carpenter's shop. He worked hard and was soon very helpful to Joseph, and even helped to teach his young brothers. Suggest what things they'd make—tables, stools, carts, etc. Ask them what they know about a carpenter's tools and build up a visual aid of the tools Jesus might have used.

   Mary's work—cooking, baking, making butter, weaving, going to the well for water—should also be discussed. Jesus' young sisters would help her. Spend some time building up a picture of the busy, happy home Jesus knew as a boy.

OPTIONAL ACTIVITIES

1. Art:
   (a) Draw, or model some carpenters' tools.
   (b) The children break up into groups to make something—baking, painting, clay, creative writing—and do the very best they can. Make a special display of their products and write above it: "Whatever your hand finds to do, do it the best you can". (a paraphrase of Ecclesiastes 9:10).

2. Hymns:
   (a) Sing: "Hands to work and feet to run" *(The Church Hymnary)*.
   (b) Learn: "Hammer and Saw".

   > Long, long ago, far, far away
   > Jesus made things with his hammer and saw
   > Rap-a-tap-tap, zip-a-zip-zip.
   > He liked to work with his hammer and saw.
   >
   > Hammer and saw, hammer and saw
   > Carpenters work with a hammer and saw
   > Hammer the nails, pound them in hard;
   > They like to build with a hammer and saw.
   >
   > *source unknown*

   (Use suitable percussion instruments.)

3. Prayer: Lord Jesus, we remember that you helped Joseph in his shop. Help us to do our best always so that we don't need to be ashamed of our work.

Lesson 3   Healing Hands

AIMS

1. To lead to some appreciation of the skills of those who care for the sick.
2. To show that Jesus cared for the ill and was able to heal them.

INTRODUCTION

Draw attention to any healing hands in your display.

SUGGESTED PROCEDURE

1. Talk about people who use their hands to care for others—mother (plaster on knee), father (whose strong hand allays their fears of the dark), nurses, doctors.

    Discuss any experiences children may have had in hospital (or of being ill at home).
2. Tell a story illustrating the healing touch of Jesus. Suitable ones included in this book are: "Jesus Heals a Little Girl"; "Blind Bartimaeus".

OPTIONAL ACTIVITIES

1. Sing: "Jesus' hands were kind hands" *(The Church Hymnary)*
2. Play at being nurses and doctors.

Lesson 4   Our Hands

AIMS

1. That the children should learn about their hands and how to care for them.
2. That they develop a responsible attitude to their use.
3. That they respond in gratitude and worship to their Creator, God.

INTRODUCTION

Refer to the fact that you've been thinking of hands and welcome comments.

SUGGESTED PROCEDURE

Say that now they are going to look at their own hands. Here are some points for consideration.

1. What do they look like?
   Encourage observation and description. There is much scope for vocabulary work (first finger, palm, etc.).
2. What can they do?
   Exercise them—clenching, holding, touching, etc. Have a collection of different articles which the children touch while their eyes are closed. They then describe what they learn about the object, using the sense of touch alone. Again there's much scope for vocabulary extension. Bring out the strength, dexterity and sensitivity of our hands. You could explain that, because of this sensitivity, blind people are able to read. Perhaps they could be shown examples of Braille writing.
3. Our dependence on our hands.
   Let them think of all the things they've used their hands for that day so far.
4. Care of our hands.
   Suggest that, since God has given us such wonderful hands, we ought to look after them. Some aspects of this are:
   cleaning them,
   protecting them from the cold,
   care in the use of tools,
   refraining from nail-biting.

bad	good
hit	give
slap	pat
punch	shake
scratch	make
steal	help
spoil	clap

5. The moral dimension

Point out that our hands affect other people. Ask for examples of the right and wrong use of one's hands.

End on a positive note, emphasizing that we can use our hands to make other people happy—and that is what God wants us to do, and will help us to do.

OPTIONAL ACTIVITIES

1. Prayer: Forgive us, oh Lord, the wrong we have done with our hands. Help us to do good and to be kind, for Jesus' sake, Amen.

2. Sing: "Hands to work and feet to run".

3. Maths: Let them compare handspans. If they stretch their hands out on a sheet of paper and put a dot at thumb and little finger, they can join the dots and compare lengths. Let them measure their desks in spans.

4. Writing: Let them think of how they can help someone today and write, "Today I am going to . . .".